WONDERFUL W

SPECIAL THANKS TO LEAH BERNSTEIN AND EVERYONE AT MOUNTAIN APPLE

Alfred Publishing Co., Inc.
16320 Roscoe Blvd., Suite 100
P.O. Box 10003
Van Nuys, CA 91410-0003
alfred.com

ISBN-10: 1-7390-4979-8
ISBN-13: 978-1-7390-4979-2

WHAT A WONDERFUL WORLD
Composed by: George D. Weiss
and Bob Thiele

I see trees of green
Red roses too
I see them bloom
For me and you
And I think to myself
What a wonderful world

I see skies of blue
And clouds of white
The bright blessed day
The dark sacred night
And I think to myself
What a wonderful world

The colors of the rainbow
So pretty in the sky
Are also on the faces
Of people goin' by
I see friends shakin' hands
Sayin', 'how do you do'
They're really sayin'
'I love you'

I hear babies cry
I watch them grow
They'll learn much more
Than I'll ever know
And I think to myself
What a wonderful world

Yes I think to myself
What a wonderful world.

`AMA`AMA
Composed by: Sam Alama

He aloha e ka i`a la
`Ai a ka `ama`ama
`Ai a ka i`a la
`Ai a ka lawalu
`Ai a ka ho`omoemoe

He aloha e ka i`a la
`Ai a ka pa`a kai
`Ai a ka i`a la
`Ai a ka `ono la
`Ai a ka sawa sawa

He aloha e ka i`a la
`Ai a ka ni`oi
`Ai a ka i`a la
`Ai a ka welawela
`Ai a ka puhipuhi

He aloha e ka i`a la
`Ai a ka `o`opu
`Ai a ka i`a la
`Aia a ka `ele`ele
`Ai a ia pake`oke`o

He aloha e ka i`a la
`Ai a ka `opihi

`Ai a ka i`a la
`Ai a ka maka la
`Ai a ka piha pohaku

Haina `ai `ia mai
`Ai ana ka puana
Hiu a ka pipi stew
Hiu a ka miki poi
Hiu a ka piha opu

I love fish
To eat mullet
To eat fish
To eat it broiled in ti leaves
Eat, then sleep

I love fish
To eat it salted
To eat fish
To eat it savory
To eat bonito broiled

I love fish
To eat with red peppers
To eat fish
Eat it steaming hot
So hot, you have to blow on it

I love fish
To eat goby fish
To eat fish
To eat seaweed
To eat to excess

I love fish
To eat limpets
To eat fish
To eat it raw
To eat until you're stuffed

Tell the story
To eat
Throw it in the beef stew
Throw it on a dab of poi
Throw in one full stomach

HENEHENE KOU `AKA
Traditional

Henehene kou `aka
Kou le`ale`a paha
He mea ma`a mau ia
For you and I

Ka`a uila mākēneki
Hō`onioni kou kino
He mea ma`a mau ia
For you and I

I Waikīkī mākou
`Au ana i ke kai
He mea ma`a mau ia
For you and I

I Kapahulu mākou
`Ai ana i ka līpo`a
He mea ma`a mau ia
For you and I

I Kaka`ako mākou
`Ai ana i ka pipi stew
He mea ma`a mau ia
For you and I

Ha`ina mai ka puana
Kou le`ale`a paha
He mea ma`a mau ia
For you and I

Merry your laughter
Your gaiety perhaps
Because it is a customary thing
For you and I

Street car
Causes to jostle my body
Because it is a customary thing
For you and I

At Waikīkī, we were
Bathing in the sea
Because it is a customary thing
For you and I

At Kapahulu, we were
Gathering/eating seaweed
Because it is a customary thing
For you and I

At Kaka`ako, we were
Eating beef stew
Because it is a customary thing
For you and I

Telling the theme
Your gaiety perhaps
Because it is a customary thing
For you and I

TWINKLE TWINKLE
LITTLE STAR
Traditional

Twinkle, twinkle, little star
How I wonder what you are
Up above the world so high
Like a diamond in the sky
Twinkle, twinkle, little star
How I wonder what you are

E KU`U MORNING DEW
Composed by: Larry Kimura
Music by: Eddie Kamae

E ku`u morning dew
Alia mai, alia mai
Maliu mai `oe i ka`u e hea nei
E kali mai `oe ia`u nei, ia`u nei
`O wau iho nō me ke aloha

Wehe mai ke alaula

`Oliliko nei līhau

E ho`ohehelo ana i nēia pāpālina

I uka o Mānā i ka `iu uhiwai

Ma laila nō kāua e pili mau ai

O my morning dew
Linger still, just a little more
Listen to what I call out to you
Wait for me, just for me
I remain yours always with love

The early glow of dawn breaks
  at the horizon
Causing the dew laden plants
  to sparkle
Making a rosey glow upon
  my cheeks
At the heights of Mānā revered
  in a cover of mist
Is where you and I shall
  remain forever

WHITE SANDY BEACH
Composed by: Willie Dann

I saw you in my dream
We were walking hand in hand
On the white sandy beach of Hawai`i

We were playin' in the sun
We were havin' so much fun
On the white sandy beach of Hawai`i

The sound of the ocean
Soothed my restless soul
The sound of the ocean
rock me all night long

Those hot long summer days
Lyin' there in the sun
On the white sandy beach of Hawai`i

Last night in my dream
I saw your face again
We were there in the sun
On the white sandy beach of Hawai`i

KALEOHANO
Composed by: Louis "Moon" Kauakahi

Kaleohano, `o Kaleohano kou inoa
Ku`u home, ku`u home
ku`u home `o Keaukaha
Kaulana `o Keaukaha

Kaleohano, `o Kaleohano kou inoa
Ku`u `āina, ku`u kulāiwi
A huli i ke kai
Kaulana `o Keaukaha

Aloha au iā Mauna Kea
i ke anu o ke ahiahi
Ho`olono, ho`olono, ho`olono
I kā leo kā makani
Keaukaha nō e ka wahi
Kaleohano, Kaleohano is your name
My home, my home
my home, Keaukaha
Famous is Keaukaha

Kaleohano, Kaleohano is your name
My land, my native land, and dashing
and receding is the sea
Famous is Keaukaha

My love is for Mauna Kea
in the cool of the evening
Listen, listen, listen
to the voice of the wind
Keaukaha indeed the place

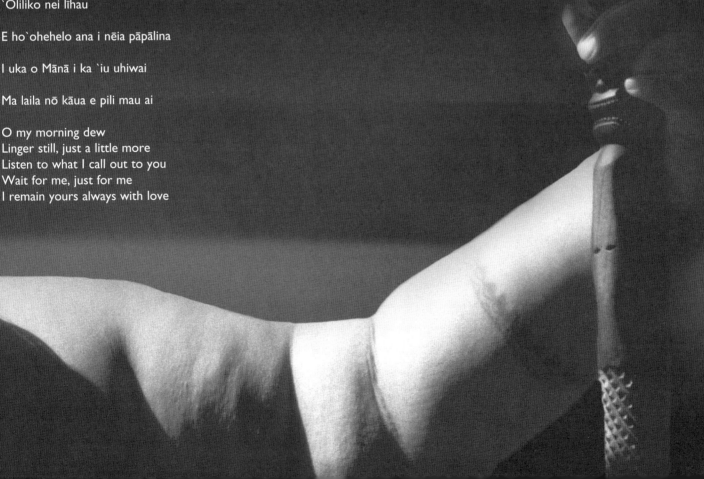

ʻKA HUILA WAI
Composed by: Alfred Alohikea

Kū wale mai no ka huila wai
Aʻohe wai iaʻu e niniu ai

He aniani kū mau ʻoe no
He hoa kūkā pū me kaua

Aloha ʻia nō Mōlīlele
I ka lele ahea i ka moana

Aloha ʻia nō o Waiʻōhinu
Ka pali lele wai a ke koae

Mai noho ʻoe a hoʻopoina
I kahi pīkake ulu maʻemaʻe

Haʻina ʻia mai ana ka puana
Aʻohe wai iʻau e niniu ai

The windmill just stands still
No water comes swirling up

You are a constant reflection of me
My companion, always conversing with me

Beloved indeed is Mōlīlele
When the clouds swirl, the ocean is stormy

Beloved is the koae bird from
The waterfall of Waiʻōhinu

Just don't you forget
This attractive peacock

Tell the refrain
No water comes swirling up

ʻŌPAE Ē
Composed by: Pilahi Paki
Music by: Irmgard ʻAluli

ʻŌpae ē
ʻŌpae hoʻi
Ua hele mai au, ua hele mai au
Na kuahine
ʻAi iā wai
ʻAi iā puhi
Nui ʻo puhi, a liʻiliʻi au
ʻAʻole loa

Pipipi ē
Pipipi hoʻi
Ua hele mai au, ua hele mai au
Na kuahine
ʻAi iā wai
ʻAi iā puhi
Nui ʻo puhi, a liʻiliʻi au
ʻAʻole loa

Pūpū e
Pūpū hoʻi

Ua hele mai au, ua hele mai au
Na kuahine
ʻAi iā wai
ʻAi iā puhi
Nui ʻo puhi, a liʻiliʻi au
ʻAʻole loa

ʻŌpaē
ʻŌpaē
I have come to you
For my sister
With whom is she?
With puhi
Puhi is large and I am tiny
No way

Pipipi
Pipipi
I have come to you
For my sister
With whom is she?
With puhi
Puhi is large and I am tiny
No way

Pūpū
Pūpū
I have come to you
For my sister
With whom is she?
With puhi
Puhi is large and I am tiny
No way

Kūpeʻe ē
Kūpeʻe hoʻi
Ua hele mai au, ua hele mai au
Na kuahine
ʻAi iā wai
ʻAi iā puhi
Nui ʻo puhi, a liʻiliʻi au
ʻAʻole loa

ʻOpihi ē
ʻOpihi hoʻi
Ua hele mai au, ua hele mai au
Na kuahine
Mai makaʻu
Naʻu e pani
I ka maka a ʻike ʻole
Kēlā puhi

Kūpeʻe
Kūpeʻe
I have come to you
For my sister
With whom is she?
With puhi
Puhi is large and I am tiny
No way

ʻOpihi
ʻOpihi
I have come to you
For my sister
Fear not

For I will cover
The eyes so that
Puhi can't see

KE ALO O IESU
Composed by: Rev. Dennis D.K. Kamakahi, ASCAP
© 1977 Naukilo Publishing Company
Lyrics reprinted by permission. All rights reserved.

E hele makou i ke alo o Iesu
E ʻike i ka nani mau loa
E hele makou i ka poli o Iesu
I ka mehana a ke aloha

Aloha ka hale kula o ka Haku
I ka lani, i ka lani kua kaʻa
I laila i ke ao o ka hoku
ʻimoʻimo
O Iesu kuʻu Haku maikaʻi

Aloha ka ʻāina o ke Akua
I ka nani, i ka nani mau loa
I laila i ke ala onaona o ka rose
O Iesu kuʻu Haku maikaʻi

Let us go to the presence of Jesus
To see everlasting beauty
Let us go to the bosom of Jesus
To the warmth of his love

Beloved is the golden house of the Lord
In heavens, in the highest heaven
There in the light
Of the twinkling star
Is Jesus, my good Lord

Beloved is the land of God
In the beauty, the everlasting beauty
There in the sweet
Scent of the rose
Is Jesus, my good Lord

ʻULILI Ē
Composed by: George Keahi and Harry Naope

ʻUlili ē ahahana ʻulili ehehene
ʻulili ahahana
ʻUlili hoʻi ehehene ʻulili ahahana
ʻulili ehehene
ʻUlili holoholo kahakai ē
O ia kai ua lana mālie

Hone ana ko leo e ʻulili ē
O kahi manu noho ʻae kai
Kiaʻi ma ka lae aʻo kekaha
ʻO ia kai ua lana mālie

Hone ana ko leo kōlea ē
Pehea ʻo Kahiki? Maikaʻi nō
ʻO ia ʻāina ʻuluwehiwehi
I hui pū ʻia me ke onaona

The sandpiper
The sandpiper returns
Sandpiper runs along the beach
Where the sea is peaceful and calm

The voice of the sandpiper is soft and sweet
Little bird who lives by the sea
Ever watchful on the beaches
Where the sea is calm

The voice of the ʻulili is soft and sweet
How are you, stranger? Very well
You grace our land
Where the sea is always calm

A HAWAIIAN LIKE ME
Composed by: Israel Kamakawiwoʻole

You may go, I'll let you go, may god bless you
You'll be mine, wherever you may be

It's a warning, to say Aloha
'cause you'll never find another Hawaiian like me
Oh no you'll never find another Hawaiian like me

You may go, I'll let you go, may god bless you
You'll be mine, wherever you may be

It's a warning, to say Aloha
'cause you'll never find another Hawaiian like me
Oh no you'll never find another Kanaka like me
Oh no you'll never find another people like us

CONTENTS

`Ama`Ama	6
E Ku`u Morning Dew	38
A Hawaiian Like Me	12
Henehene Kou `Aka	16
Ka Huila Wai	43
Kaleohano	24
Ke Alo O Iesu	50
`Ōpae Ē	55
Over The Rainbow	60
Twinkle Twinkle Little Star	65
`Ulili Ē	70
What A Wonderful World	28
White Sandy Beach	34

'AMA'AMA

Words and Music by
SAM ALAMA

*Guitar/Uke: IZ tuned his ukulele to GCEA, the same as the top 4 strings of a guitar with the capo at the 5th fret.
Guitarists: For this song, capo at the 7th fret and play indicated 4-string chords. Ukulele: Capo 2.

'Ama'Ama - 6 - 1
29030

3.4. He a - lo - ha sa - wa.____

(Inst. solo ad lib....

Verses 5 & 6:

`Ama`Ama - 6 - 4
29030

English Translation:

I love fish,
To eat mullet,
To eat fish,
To eat it broiled in ti leaves,
Eat, then sleep.

I love fish,
To eat it salted,
To eat fish,
To eat it savory,
To eat bonito broiled.

I love fish,
To eat with red peppers,
To eat fish,
Eat it steaming hot,
So hot you have to blow on it.

I love fish,
To eat goby fish,
To eat fish,
To eat seaweed,
To eat to excess.

I love fish,
To eat limpets,
To eat fish,
To eat it raw,
To eat until you are stuffed.

Tell the story,
To eat,
Throw it in the beef stew,
Throw it on a dab of poi
Throw in one full stomach.

A HAWAIIAN LIKE ME

Words and Music by
ISRAEL KAMAKAWIWO'OLE

*Guitar/Uke: IZ tuned his ukulele to GCEA, the same as the top 4 strings of a guitar with the capo at the 5th fret.
Guitarists: Capo at the 5th fret and play indicated 4-string chords. Ukulele: Play as indicated.

This arrangement © 2007 MOUNTAIN APPLE COMPANY HAWAI'I,
1330 Ala Moana Blvd., Suite 001, Honolulu, HI 96814

never find another Hawaiian like me.

2. You may me.

It's a

warn - ing___ to say, "A - lo -

ha," 'cause you'll nev - er find___ an - oth - er Ha - wai - ian like

HENEHENE KOU `AKA

TRADITIONAL

*Guitar/Uke: IZ tuned his ukulele to GCEA, the same as the top 4 strings of a guitar with the capo at the 5th fret.
Guitarists: For this song, capo at the 6th fret and play indicated 4-string chords. Ukulele: Capo 1.

This arrangement © 1993 MOUNTAIN APPLE COMPANY HAWAI'I,
1330 Ala Moana Blvd., Suite 001, Honolulu, HI 96814
All Rights Reserved   Used by Permission
www.mountainapplecompany.com

20

sev - en and eight, nine, ten, e - lev - en a - gain.

English Translation:
Merry your laughter,
Your gaiety perhaps,
Because it is a customary thing
For you and I.

Street car (magnetic electric bus)
Causes to jostle my body,
Because it is a customary thing
For you and I.

At Waikiki, we were
Bathing (swimming) in the sea,
Because it is a customary thing
For you and I.

At Kapahulu, we were
Gathering/eating seaweed,
Because it is a customary thing
For you and I.

At Kaka`ako we were
Eating beef stew,
Because it is a customary thing
For you and I.

Telling the theme,
Your gaiety perhaps,
Because it is a customary thing,
For you and I.

KALEOHANO

Words and Music by
LOUIS "MOON" KAUAKAHI

*Suggested chord frames, no guitar or uke on recording.

Kaleohano - 4 - 1
29030

lo - no, i kā le - o kā ma - ka - ni. Kea - u - ka - ha nō e ka

wa - hi.

Verse 4:

lo - ha au iā Mau-na Kea,_____ i ke a-nu o ke a - a-hi - hi. Ho-`o-

4. A -

English Translation:
Kaleohano, Kaleohano is your name,
My home, my home, my home, Keaukaha,
Famous is Keaukaha.

Kaleohano, Kaleohano is your name,
My land, my native land, and dashing and receding is the sea,
Famous is Keaukaha.

My love is for Mauna Kea, in the cool of the evening,
Listen, listen, listen to the voice of the wind,
Keaukaha is indeed the place.

WHAT A WONDERFUL WORLD

Words and Music by
GEORGE DAVID WEISS
and BOB THIELE

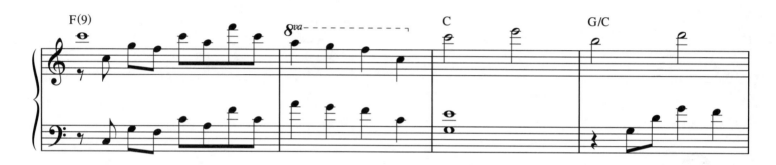

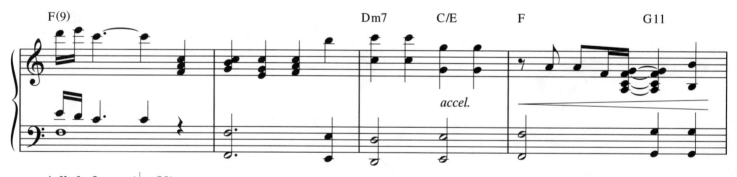

*Guitar/Uke: IZ tuned his ukulele to GCEA, the same as the top 4 strings of a guitar with the capo at the 5th fret.
Guitarists: Capo at the 5th fret and play indicated 4-string chords. Ukulele: Play as indicated.

What a Wonderful World - 6 - 1
29030

than we'll know. And I think to my-self,   what a won-der-ful

world,   what a won-der-ful world.

WHITE SANDY BEACH

Words and Music by
WILLY DANN

* Guitar/Uke: IZ tuned his ukulele to GCEA, the same as the top 4 strings of a guitar with the capo at the 5th fret.
Guitarists: Capo at the 5th fret and play indicated 4-string chords. Ukulele: Play as indicated.

36

White Sandy Beach - 4 - 3
29030

Verse 3:
Those hot long summer days,
Lying there in the sun
On a white sandy beach of Hawaii.
(To Chorus:)

E KU'U MORNING DEW

Words by
LARRY L. KIMURA

Music by
EDDIE KAMAE

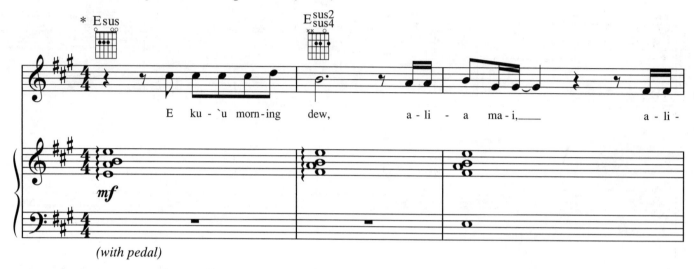

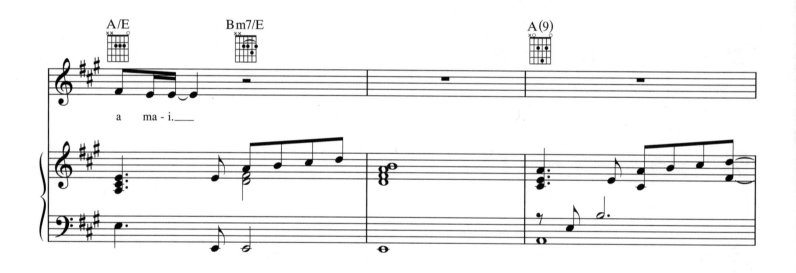

*Suggested chord frames, no guitar or uke on recording.

E Ku'U Morning Dew - 5 - 1
29030

Verses 1 & 2:

1. E ku -`u morn - ing
2. We - he mai ke a -

(with pedal)

dew, a - li - a ma - i,___ a - li - a ma - i.___
lau - la,___ `o - li - li - ko___ nei li - hau.

Ma - li - u mai `o - e,___ i ka -`u___ e he - a
E ho - `o - he - lo a - na,___ i nē - ia___ pā - pā - li -

Verse 3:

English Translation:
O, my morning dew,
Linger still, just a little more.
Listen to what I call out to you.
Wait for me, just for me,
I remain yours always with love.

The early glow of dawn breaks at the horizon,
'Causing the dew-laden plants to sparkle.
Making a rosey glow across my cheeks.
At the heights of Mana revered in a cover of mist
Is where you and I shall remain forever.

KA HUILA WAI

Words and Music by
ALFRED ALOHIKEA

*Guitar/Uke: IZ tuned his ukulele to GCEA, the same as the top 4 strings of a guitar with the capo at the 5th fret.
Guitarists: Capo at the 5th fret and play indicated 4-string chords. Ukulele: Play as indicated.

English Translation:
The windmill just stands still,
No water comes swirling up.
You are a constant reflection of me,
My companion, always conversing with me.
Beloved indeed is Molilele,
When the clouds swirl, the ocean is stormy.
Beloved is the koae bird from
The waterfall of Wai ohinu.
Just don't you forget
This attractive peacock.
Tell the refrain,
No water comes swirling up.

KA ALO O IESU

Words and Music by
DENNIS KAMAKAHI

* Guitar/Uke: IZ tuned his ukulele to GCEA, the same as the top 4 strings of a guitar with the capo at the 5th fret.
Guitarists: Capo at the 5th fret and play indicated 4-string chords. Ukulele: Play as indicated.

Chorus 1:

Guitar Solo:

English Translation:

Let us go to the presence of Jesus
To see everlasting beauty.
Let us go to the bosom of Jesus
To the warmth of his love.

Beloved is the golden house of the Lord
In heavens, in the highest heaven.
There in the light of the twinking star
Is Jesus, my good Lord.

Beloved is the land of God
In the beauty, the everlasting beauty.
There in the sweet scent of the rose
Is Jesus, my good Lord.

`Ōpae Ē

Words and Music by
IRMGARD ALULI

* Performed on guitar, no capo. (No uke.)

`Ōpae Ē - 5 - 1
29030

au,   u-a he le mai__ au.   Na ku-a-hi - ne.   5. Mai ma

Chorus 5:

ka `u,_____   na-`u e pa-ni.___   I__ ka

ma-ka, a__ `i ke__ `o-le kē - lā__ pu - hi.

Slowly

Verse 3:
Kūpe`e ē, kūpe`e ho`i
Ua hele mai au, ua hele mai au
Na kuahine.
(To Chorus:)

Verse 4:
Pipipi ē, pipipi ho`i
Ua hele mai, ua hele mai au
Na kuahine.

English Translation:
Ōpaē, ōpaē.
I have come to you for my sister.
With whom is she?
With puhi
Puhi is large and I am tiny
No way.

Pūpū, pūpū.
I have come to you for my sister.
With whom is she?
With puhi
Puhi is large and I am tiny
No way.

Pipipi, pipipi,
I have come to you for my sister.
With whom is she?
With puhi
Puhi is large and I am tiny
No way.

Kūpe`e, kūpe`e,
I have come to you for my sister.
With whom is she?
With puhi
Puhi is large and I am tiny
No way.

`Opihi, `opihi,
I have come to you for my sister.
Fear not
For I will cover
The eyes so that
Puhi can't see.

*Note: The following are the English names of the sea creatures mentioned in this song: ōpae - shrimp; Pūpū - marine shell; Pipipi - small mollusk; Kūpe`e - marine snail; Puhi - eel; `Opihi - limpet.

OVER THE RAINBOW

Lyric by
E.Y. Harburg

Music by
HAROLD ARLEN

*Guitar/Uke: IZ tuned his ukulele to GCEA, the same as the top 4 strings of a guitar with the capo at the 5th fret.
Guitarists: Capo at the 5th fret and play indicated 4-string chords. Ukulele: Play as indicated.

Over the Rainbow - 5 - 1
29030

62

TWINKLE TWINKLE LITTLE STAR

Traditional

* Suggested chord frames, no guitar or uke on recording.

Twinkle Twinkle Little Star - 5 - 3
29030

68

Twinkle Twinkle Little Star - 5 - 5
29030

`ULILI Ē

Words and Music by
GEORGE KEAHI and HARRY NAOPE

*Guitar/Uke: IZ tuned his ukulele to GCEA, the same as the top 4 strings of a guitar with the capo at the 5th fret.
Guitarists: Capo at the 5th fret and play indicated 4-string chords. Ukulele: Play as indicated.

`Ulili Ē - 7 - 1
29030

Verse 2:

ē,_____ `U - li - li  ho - `i.

English Translation:
The voice of the sandpiper is soft and sweet;
Little bird who lives by the sea,
Ever watchful on the beaches
Where the sea is calm.

The sandpiper,
The sandpiper returns.
Sandpiper runs along the beach
Where the sea is peaceful and calm.

The voice of the `ulili is soft and sweet.
How are you, stranger? Very well.
You grace our land
Where the sea is always calm.